Texts and Human Experiences

A Skills based approach to the Common Module HSC English 2019–2023

Bruce Pattinson

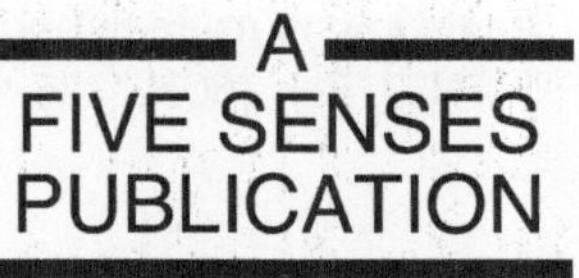

Five Senses Education Pty Ltd
2/195 Prospect Highway
Seven Hills 2147
New South Wales
Australia

First Published 2018. Revised and updated October 2018.

Pattinson, Bruce
Texts and Human Experiences: A Skills Based Approach to the Common Module
ISBN 978-1-76032-235-9

2018 10 15

INTRODUCTION TO THE COMMON MODULE: TEXTS AND HUMAN EXPERIENCES

This book is explicitly designed to help you in understanding the Common Module: *Texts and Human Experiences* for the 2019–23 Higher School Certificate in New South Wales. This course is a common module for Advanced, Standard and English Studies courses and the NSW Education Standards Authority (NESA) has made it mandatory in the course requirements.

The book begins by giving you an introductory understanding of the topic 'Human Experience' with questions designed to extend and develop a complete, actionable knowledge. To assist we have developed a series of activities to increase awareness of specific facets of this complex area.

The next section is designed to help prepare you for the type of questions you will find in the first section of Paper One for the HSC. It will consist of four to five short-answer questions based on stimulus material and / or unseen texts which relate to the Common Module. You will be guided through literary and visual techniques and then offered a series of sample stimuli and questions to answer.

Finally, we tackle the essay and the use of related textual material. The second section of Paper One of the HSC will include a question which requires a sustained response based on your set text. It may also include stimulus and / or unseen texts.

This section gives both guidance and extended annotated examples of the types of texts that could be used to reinforce the key ideas in your set text. The basics of the essay are covered as is the development of the opening paragraph.

You do not have to use the book from front to back but you can pick and choose exercises as needed. This book will develop your skills and ideas about the Common Module and I hope it will expand your understanding so that this will translate into improved results.

I wish you all the best in your studies.

Bruce Pattinson

CONTENTS

Common Module:
Texts and Human Experiences

What is the Common Module?

The Common Module set for the 2019–23 HSC is *Texts and Human Experiences*. It is compulsory to study this topic as prescribed by NESA and it is common to all three English courses. Remember you will be learning how texts reveal individual and collective human experiences. There are no right or wrong answers in this module – it is about how you see and interpret material and engage with it.

In the Common Module you will be analysing one prescribed text and a range of short texts that are related to the idea of human experiences. You will analyse texts not only to investigate the ideas they represent about human experiences but also how they deliver these ideas. This means you will be looking closely at the techniques a composer uses to represent his / her messages and shape meaning.

Specifically you will look at one set text from the following list:

- Doerr, Anthony, *All the Light We Cannot See*
- Lohrey, Amanda, *Vertigo*
- Orwell, George, *Nineteen Eighty-Four*
- Parrett, Favel, *Past the Shallows*
- Dobson, Rosemary 'Young Girl at a Window', 'Over the Hill', 'Summer's End', 'The Conversation', 'Cock Crow', 'Amy Caroline', 'Canberra Morning'
- Slessor, Kenneth 'Wild Grapes', 'Gulliver', 'Out of Time', 'Vesper-Song of the Reverend Samuel Marsden', 'William Street', 'Beach Burial'
- Harrison, Jane, *Rainbow's End*
- Miller, Arthur, *The Crucible*
- Shakespeare, William, *The Merchant of Venice*
- Winton, Tim, *The Boy Behind the Curtain* Chapters: 'Havoc: A Life in Accidents', 'Betsy', 'Twice on Sundays', 'The Wait and the Flow', 'In the Shadow of the Hospital', 'The Demon Shark', 'Barefoot in the Temple of Art'
- Yousafzai, Malala & Lamb, Christina, *I am Malala*
- Daldry, Stephen, *Billy Elliot*
- O'Mahoney, Ivan, *Go Back to Where You Came From* – Series 1, Episodes 1, 2 and 3 and *The Response*
- Walker, Lucy, *Waste Land*

NESA has mandated that students must study a related text as part of the common module, and that this should be part of their in-school assessment. However there is **no longer** a requirement to write about a related text in the HSC examination itself.

In your own words describe what you are required to do in the Common Module: Texts and Human Experiences to meet the requirements of the course.

Which text are you studying? What type of text is it?

List THREE Other Related Texts that you can use as resources. To help you we have included an annotated list of a variety of texts at the end of this workbook as a starting point.

What does NESA require for the Common Module?

The NESA documentation of the Common Module: Texts and Human Experiences states that students:

- deepen their understanding of how texts represent individual and collective human experiences;
- examine how texts represent human qualities and emotions associated with, or arising from, these experiences;
- appreciate, explore, interpret, analyse and evaluate the ways language is used to shape these representations in a range of texts in a variety of forms, modes and media;
- explore how texts may give insight into the anomalies, paradoxes and inconsistencies in human behaviour and motivations, inviting the responder to see the world differently, to challenge assumptions, ignite new ideas or reflect personally;
- may also consider the role of storytelling throughout time to express and reflect particular lives and cultures;
- by responding to a range of texts, further develop skills and confidence using various literary devices, language concepts, modes and media to formulate a considered response to texts;
- study one prescribed text and a range of short texts that provide rich opportunities to further explore representations of human experiences illuminated in texts;
- make increasingly informed judgements about how aspects of these texts, for example context, purpose, structure, stylistic and grammatical features, and form shape meaning;
- select one related text and draw from personal experience to make connections between themselves, the world of the text and their wider world;
- by responding and composing throughout the module, further develop a repertoire of skills in comprehending, interpreting and analysing complex texts;
- examine how different modes and media use visual, verbal and/or digital language elements;
- communicate ideas using figurative language to express universal themes and evaluative language to make informed judgements about texts; and
- further develop skills in using metalanguage, correct grammar and syntax to analyse language and express a personal perspective about a text.

If this is what is required by NESA we need to examine the concept of human experience carefully so we can adequately respond in these ways. I would recommend that you read the complete document which is on the NESA website and can be downloaded in Word or Adobe. Understanding this document is an important step in handling the textual material within the guidelines required — remember you are reading for a purpose and should make notes and highlight ideas as you read so that you can develop these ideas later.

Find the English Stage 6 Prescriptions 2019–2023 document on the NESA website and download it. Write the URL below.

In your own words write what you think you need to do to be confident in completing Paper One successfully. What are some of the skills required?

List ONE area of weakness you think you might have and how you can develop your skills in that area.

Texts and Human Experiences: Vocabulary

The terminologies listed are words you need to be familiar with. You should read the list carefully and if you are unfamiliar with the word and its meaning find the meaning of the word and how it is used. Some words are defined in the English Syllabus which can be found online at the NESA website while the others can be found in any online dictionary. Try to find the meaning in your own words and be mindful of the context — some words have subtle changes in meaning depending on the context.

General Terms

individual

collective

human qualities

emotions

anomalies

paradoxes

inconsistencies

behaviour

motivation

assumptions

English Terminology

texts

represent

appreciate

explore

interpret

analyse

evaluate

form

mode

media

metalanguage

responder

reflect

context

purpose

structure

stylistic features

grammatical features

repertoire

figurative

universal themes

perspective

Understanding the Common Module

What are Human Experiences?

The concept of Human Experiences is at the heart of the Common Module.

Human Experiences are experiences of individuals or a group of people (eg a family, society, or nation) in life. There are a very wide range of human experiences which include but go beyond this list:

- feelings or reactions (momentary or long term): love, hate, anger, joy, fear, disgust
- key milestones or stages: birth, childhood, adulthood, marriage, divorce, death
- culture, belonging and identity
- conformity and rebellion
- innocence and guilt, justice
- freedom and repression
- education, vocation, work, sport, leisure
- attraction to a person, idea, group or cause
- opposition to an idea, cause, political system
- religious faith or belief
- extreme events such as an earthquake, avalanche, tsuanami
- regular events such as walking, eating, singing, dancing, discussing ideas.

The word *experience* seems innately connected to the human condition and it is something we have each day whether a mundane experience that is repetitive or something new and dramatic which offers challenges and rewards. Experiences can vary greatly in their impact on individuals, groups and countries. One example might be a war that is a negative experience on a whole population while we may experience the wonder of medicine with a new vaccine for a deadly disease that saves millions of people. We need to note that the module asks for 'experiences' ...we are a combination of different experiences and each has a varying impact. One person's problem is another's challenge depending on perspective, skill set, previous experience and ability.

Experiences are widespread and often shared: this is why people tell their stories and these shared experiences form part of our cultural heritage. These experiences often inform, warn and teach across entire cultural groups and many stories are shared across cultures.

Defining Human Experiences

Now let's attempt to define what human experiences are and shape them into a more coherent and easily understood framework so we can begin our investigation at a basic level of understanding before moving into more complex analysis and looking at how the texts illuminate our understanding of the term.

Dictionary.com defines the term experience as:

noun

1. a particular instance of personally encountering or undergoing something:
2. the process or fact of personally observing, encountering, or undergoing something:
3. the observing, encountering, or undergoing of things generally as they occur in the course of time:
   to learn from experience; the range of human experience.
4. knowledge or practical wisdom gained from what one has observed, encountered, or undergone:
   a man of experience.
5. *Philosophy.* the totality of the cognitions given by perception; all that is perceived, understood, and remembered.

verb (used with object), **experienced, experiencing.**

6. to have experience of; meet with; undergo; feel:
   to experience nausea.
7. to learn by experience.

Idioms

8. **experience religion;** to undergo a spiritual conversion by which one gains or regains faith in God.

Obviously there are a number of definitions according to context, but all are applicable to our study in some shape or form, as the range of human experiences is so vast. The search for the 'new experience' has driven much of the development of people, groups, cultures and nations over past millennia. New experiences are always met with excitement and often trepidation as to what change they might bring.

Think historically about how people have reacted to change. It can cause great upheavals in society, with violent reactions while other changes brought through various experiences are welcomed and may change how people live and comprehend the world. Experiences affect us emotionally in many cases rather than logically and when we deal emotionally behaviours become unpredictable. This causes the paradoxes, anomalies and inconsistencies mentioned in the rubric. If we were logical beings the world would be an easier place.

These definitions all point to the fact that the memory is the key to experience. The experience is stored in memory and drawn upon when the circumstances are repeated or closely mimicked so we can deal with them – hopefully better than on the initial experience.

Experiences can come in many ways and the synonyms listed below for experience help us to understand the concept even further. They assist in defining how an experience can arise:

Synonyms

actions
background
contacts
involvement
know-how
maturity
participation
patience
practice
reality
sense
skill
struggle
training

understanding
wisdom
acquaintances
actuality
caution
combat
doings
empiricism
evidence
existences
exposures
familiarity
intimacy
inwardness

judgment
observation
perspicacity
practicality
proofs
savoir-faire
seasonings
sophistication
strife
trials
worldliness
forebearance

http://www.thesaurus.com/browse/experience?s=t

These synonyms show partly the vast array of words that our language has created around this concept, and also shows how important it is in the human psyche. We, as humans, want to experience. Now we will look at some examples of experiences and examine how they can impact. It is also important to remember that experiences do not have to be positive. You might experience a huge problem, a bereavement, a car accident, an unwelcome relationship or something totally bizarre that rocks your world. There can be a more opaque side to any experience that may need to be addressed.

The whole aim of this Common Module is to examine the text closely but also relate it to the concept of human experiences and decide how examining it in this way enables us to better understand both the text and the concept of humanity.

It is important that you unpack what each text you study shows you about human experiences and what ideas / themes arise from those experiences. Formulate your own ideas about the text.

Read the NESA Stage 6 document called *English Stage 6: Annotations of selected texts prescribed for the Higher School Certificate 2019-23* for the set text you are studying. This document offers insights into the way each particular text should be examined by outlining key ideas and areas for clarification.

Go back to the list of words on page 9 as these show you the types of experiences and effects that you will be studying. If you didn't find the meanings of these words then – do it now. This is one of the key elements to understanding what you study and how to convey that information effectively.

Human experiences and ways of experiencing vary due to individual circumstance and these experiences can change many things about individual lives, communities and the world. When we examine the concept of human experience in relation to a text, we need to examine the assumptions or biases we bring to it as well as how experiencing the text itself may change us and how we view things. The text may challenge and confront how we view the human experience or we may have preconceived ideas that make it more difficult for this to happen.

Students can also think about their own 'personal experience to make connections between themselves, the world of the text and their wider world.' Examining and enjoying any text is an experience in itself but it is what we take away from the text and apply that is the crucial aspect. That is not to say that every text will be enjoyed or offer a human experience that is significant either positively or negatively. Some texts may not personally engage you and that is fine. This is especially so when you begin to look for other related material that links to *Texts and Human Experiences*. We recommend that you find examples of texts that link but also personally appeal to you so that you can relate empathetically with them.

Write about ONE experience you have had in your life. It doesn't have to be anything world shattering but write about an interesting experience or event. It might be a trip to a new place, meeting new people or overcoming adversity. Think about your emotions, behaviour and perspective as you reflect on how that experience affected you.

Clarify Your Ideas

Define the concept of texts and human experiences in your own words. This is the definition you will use in the examination and your assessment tasks so make it relevant and clear to YOU!

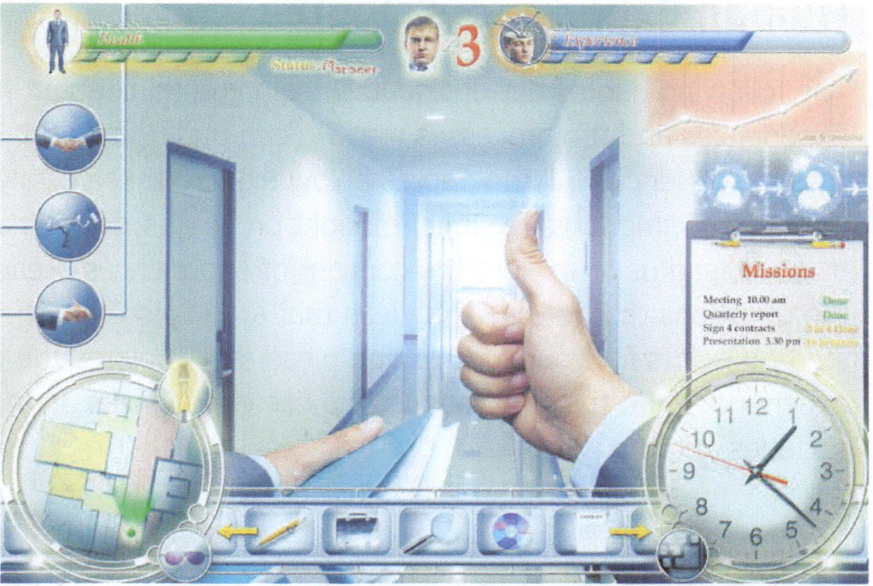

You cannot be wrong if you can support your ideas with evidence, especially if it is from a text.

Human Experiences Quotes

The following quotes are designed to help you think about how we make human experiences and the processes that we can undergo by thinking about and having these experiences. All the quotes below explore these catalysts and present us with a variety of emotions, feelings, thought processes, and initial steps that we can take that will lead us to explore the concept of experiences. Read the quotes and answer the questions that follow. The ideas that are explored in these quotes can be good starting points for your own writing piece that explores the concept of human experiences and the implications of these experiences on individuals, groups, societies and the world.

The marvellous richness of human experience would lose something of rewarding joy if there were no limitations to overcome. The hilltop hour would not be half so wonderful if there were no dark valleys to traverse.

Helen Keller

Do you agree with Helen Keller's view? Why or why not?

People are afraid of themselves, of their own reality; their feelings most of all. People talk about how great love is, but that's bull. Love hurts. Feelings are disturbing. People are taught that pain is evil and dangerous. How can they deal with love if they're afraid to feel? Pain is meant to wake us up. People try to hide their pain. But they're wrong. Pain is something to carry, like a radio. You feel your strength in the experience of pain. It's all in how you carry it. That's what matters. Pain is a feeling. Your feelings are a part of you. Your own reality. If you feel ashamed of them, and hide them, you're letting society destroy your reality. You should stand up for your right to feel your pain.

Jim Morrison

Do you agree with Jim Morrison's view of people and the need for pain in our lives? Think about the concept of contrasts in human experiences and how people react to these.

Above all, don't lie to yourself. The man who lies to himself and listens to his own lie comes to a point that he cannot distinguish the truth within him, or around him, and so loses all respect for himself and for others. And having no respect he ceases to love.

Fyodor Dostoyevsky

How true is this? Do people lie to themselves as a form of controlling experiences?

Your work is going to fill a large part of your life, and the only way to be truly satisfied is to do what you believe is great work. And the only way to do great work is to love what you do. If you haven't found it yet, keep looking. Don't settle. As with all matters of the heart, you'll know when you find it. And, like any great relationship, it just gets better and better as the years roll on. So keep looking until you find it. Don't settle.

Steve Jobs

What is Jobs saying in this quote about work as part of human experiences?

There's a power in what we hold as artists, and part of that comes with responsibility ... to share the human experience and really allow that to be seen.

Tracee Ellis Ross

What type of artists share human experience through their work? Can you think of a piece of art, drama, theatre or a piece of writing which captures human experience well? Give details.

____

____

____

____

____

Courage. Kindness. Friendship. Character. These are the qualities that define us as human beings, and propel us, on occasion, to greatness."

R.J. Palacio, Wonder

From your own experience, talk about how these qualities have impacted your life. How does our interaction with others shape our experiences?

____

____

____

____

____

____

____

____

There are two basic motivating forces: fear and love. When we are afraid, we pull back from life. When we are in love, we open to all that life has to offer with passion, excitement, and acceptance. We need to learn to love ourselves first, in all our glory and our imperfections. If we cannot love ourselves, we cannot fully open to our ability to love others or our potential to create. Evolution and all hopes for a better world rest in the fearlessness and open-hearted vision of people who embrace life.

John Lennon

What do these TWO texts suggest about openness as an important aspect of human experiences?

You'll learn, as you get older, that rules are made to be broken. Be bold enough to live life on your terms, and never, ever apologise for it. Go against the grain, refuse to conform, take the road less travelled instead of the well-beaten path. Laugh in the face of adversity, and leap before you look. Dance as though EVERYBODY is watching. March to the beat of your own drummer. And stubbornly refuse to fit in.

Mandy Hale

There's a loneliness that only exists in one's mind. The loneliest moment in someone's life is when they are watching their whole world fall apart, and all they can do is stare blankly.

F. Scott Fitzgerald

Sometimes people think they know you. They know a few facts about you, and they piece you together in a way that makes sense to them. And if you don't know yourself very well, you might even believe that they are right. But the truth is, that isn't you. That isn't you at all.

Leila Sales

Choose ONE of the quotes above and write why you chose it and what it says to you about human experiences.

Types of Human Experiences

Before we begin let's find out what we know and build on that. In the space below list different types of human experience and an example of each.

1 ____

2 ____

3 ____

4 ____

5 ____

Now we will move into examining some different types of human experiences and then develop some ideas that can be moulded into something original to use with your text and in the essay.

First we will try to clarify for you what it is to be human so that we can understand the importance of experiences to people and how these experiences make us who we are: individually and collectively. Think about how you might define the term 'humanity' and what qualities you would give to that definition.

Try to have this definition and analysis clearly in your mind as we proceed to look at the various types of human experiences we have on a personal level.

Individual Human Experience

The idea of personal experiences is a popular and pervasive concept, especially in the literature of some cultures. The recording of personal experiences as a means of sharing wisdom or more mundane daily tasks is part of human nature, and we record and relate these experiences frequently. Experiences are recorded and relayed in many ways: we tell oral stories in both anecdotal and formal ways, we write, draw, sing and photograph our way into history (or not). Look at the proliferation of social media in this current century as people record their daily, even hourly, experiences for all to see. We record the most trivial details of our lives for likes and followers while the real world passes us by. Human experiences affect us on a daily basis and some experiences influence our lives and the way we live them.

Individuals seek to achieve experiences in a variety of ways. Some seek more and more extreme experiences to test themselves against the world; others limit their experiences, while most people prefer the familiar and don't actively seek new experiences. Individuals, it must be remembered, also see experiences in different ways and the same experience may have a very different impact on individuals. The one thing we can be certain about is that experiences are part of humanity, and even the most limited of us have them. Many of these experiences also come from interaction with others and as noted, we also like to share these experiences. Experiences are what define us in many ways and this is what makes us human.

We are going to look at four specific ways that experiences can influence us as people over the next few pages. These are physical, psychological, emotional and intellectual experiences, and many experiences are a combination of these. Before we go into more detail let's complete a few questions to firm up our ideas.

In your own words define the term individual experience.

____

____

____

____

List some ways people have personal experiences.

Give an example of an individual human experience you have found in your research/studies.

Is there an example of an individual human experience in your set text? If so give an example and page reference.

Physical Experience

The concept of a physical experience is tied to the human experience and is part of the collective experience as well. Individuals seek physical experiences to test themselves against nature and other individuals, often as part of trials and rituals associated with cultural aspects of being integrated into a community. In modern times individuals have sought to test themselves with extreme sports and explorations into the harshest conditions and even space. Physical experiences can also change the way we see the world and others because of the chemical changes these experiences have on our bodies and mind. Physical experiences are often challenges, and part of the experience is overcoming adversity. These physical challenges are often celebrated, as in the case of sports, but can also offer challenges if the experience is a negative one (such as an accident or disease). Physical experiences are also often quite public, and thus have permeated our societies in both their execution and how they are perceived. These physical experiences, even if experienced vicariously, have become popular across cultures and celebrated. Think of examples for yourself, but most competitive sports offer examples.

Bruce Lee extends the concept of the physical experience into all aspects of life and that's what we will look at next in our analysis of human experiences – *"If you always put limit on everything you do, physical or anything else, it will spread into your work and into your life. There are no limits. There are only plateaus, and you must not stay there, you must go beyond them."*

In your own words, what is a physical experience?

List some ways people have physical experiences.

Give an example of a physical experience you have found in your research/studies.

Is there an example of a physical experience in your set text? If so give an example and page reference.

Psychological Experience

The idea of a psychological experience is tied into many of the abstract ideas that people experience, and can lead to a discussion of what is normal psychology. From the earliest times humans have attempted to alter their psychology through a number of experiences. On a simple level this can be a drug that changes the person's or group's perspective on reality. Examples of this might be alcohol or marijuana, but cultural groups also use various substances to share group experiences. This can be seen in Native American cultures with peyote. In more modern times prescription drugs that are mood altering have been used to minimise the symptoms of psychiatric illnesses (such as depression) and these mood altering drugs are common and legal. Others attempt to alter their psychology by seeing 'specialists' in this area, while others may act out their psychology leading to social and criminal issues. When discussing the human experience psychology is a key issue and will form a part of most studies of experience. When taken too far this search for a new psychological experience can be harmful (such as an addiction).

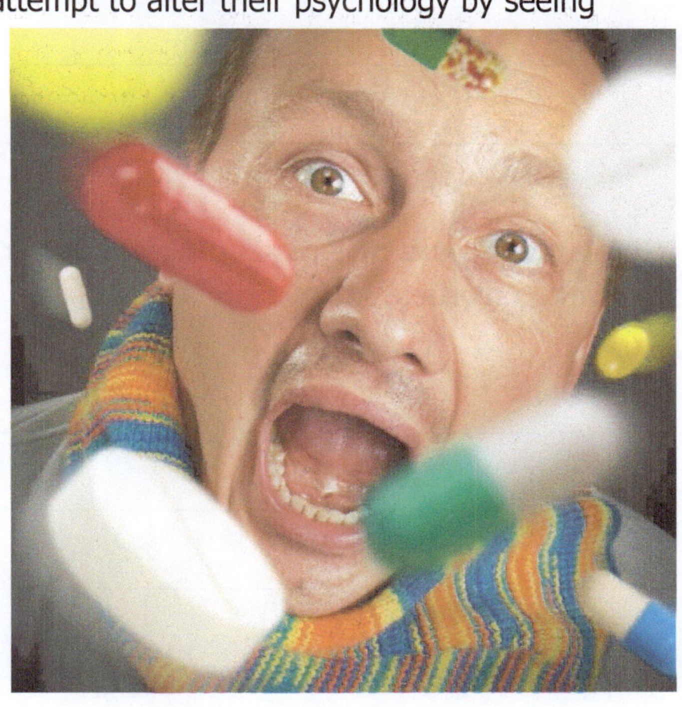

Carl Jung, the famous psychologist comments on the problems of addiction on human experiences, stating clearly that excess can be an issue: "Every form of addiction is bad, no matter whether the narcotic be alcohol, morphine or idealism."

In your own words, what is a psychological experience?

List some ways people have psychological experiences.

Give an example of a psychological experience you have found in your research/studies.

Is there an example of a psychological experience in your set text? If so give an example and page reference.

Emotional Experience

Robert Plutchik's theory says that the eight basic emotions are:

- Fear → feeling afraid.
- Anger → feeling angry. A stronger word for anger is *rage.*
- Sadness → feeling sad. Other words are *sorrow, grief* (a stronger feeling, for example when someone has died) or *depression* (feeling sad for a long time). Some people think depression is a different emotion.
- Joy → feeling happy. Other words are *happiness, gladness.*
- Disgust → feeling something is wrong or nasty
- Trust → a positive emotion; admiration is stronger; acceptance is weaker
- Anticipation → in the sense of looking forward positively to something which is going to happen. Expectation is more neutral.

https://simple.wikipedia.org/wiki/List_of_emotions

Emotions are the strongest drivers of human experience and form lasting aspects of any experience. Think about breaking up with someone you love and the emotions that drive behaviours in this situation. People have all sorts of extreme behaviours under the influence of emotions, and these experiences are often the ones recorded and are those which influence us most. Think about the role emotions play in our lives and the range of emotions from the list above. Consider how much emotions affect our life experiences, how they influence our decisions which decide our experiences. On a larger level, consider how they affect others' decisions, which lead to experiences that seriously change our lives (such as politicians going to war).

In your own words, what is an emotional experience?

List some ways people have emotional experiences.

Give an example of an emotional experience you have found in your research/studies or in your own life.

Is there an example of an emotional experience in your set text? If so give an example and page reference.

Intellectual Experience

The concept of an intellectual experience is linked to decisions and experiences we have based on analysis and logic rather than the emotional choices we saw in the previous section. These intellectual experiences have changed the way we live and how we have seen our world. These experiences have affected the way we as humans have altered our world to suit our needs, and lead to all the great advances in human society and thus experiences. Changes in our ideas, beliefs etc. alter the way we interact with the world, and often these intellectual changes come at great cost. Think of the time in Europe when the Church dominated and stopped scientific advances by calling them heresy/ witchcraft. Open societies are more open to new ideas and this is what has fastened the pace of intellectual experiences as dominant ideologies fall away. Intellectual advances may not have the excitement that the other types produce, but perhaps they have a more lasting impact on people, societies and the world in general. Ideas are powerful experiences and people hold beliefs strongly.

Immanuel Kant stated that: "experience without theory is blind, but theory without experience is mere intellectual play". Consider this statement in light of what we have learnt about human experiences. Are they a combination of many factors or can we isolate experiences into simple forms? After the next few questions we are going to examine how humans respond to experiences and how they record them.

In your own words, what is an intellectual experience?

____

____

____

____

____

List some ways people have intellectual experiences.

Give an example of an intellectual experience you have found in your research/studies or one you have had personally.

Is there an example of an intellectual experience in your set text? If so give an example and page reference.

Impact of Human Experiences

Human experiences impact on many levels as we have seen in our previous discussions. On an individual level we can have changes in our assumptions about the world and people around us; we can ingest new ideas and have these open new vistas of productivity and performance. We can also reflect and build on these experiences to ensure that they are even more meaningful to our lives. Behaviours towards others and the way we respond to the world can manifest themselves in new and different responses. An example might be that through adverse experiences we can build resilience so the next negative experience isn't as traumatic and we accept it for what it is. Experiences also teach us new behaviours on a very physical level – if you burn yourself once on a flame you learn not to do it again (hopefully).

The impact of human experiences can also be shared in groups and societies. Firstly, let's examine some group dynamics that can be affected by human experiences. Groups share experiences and adapt and develop behaviours that impact on the group as a whole. Think about the notorious 'bonding' sessions sporting teams have that unite them in a common goal. Think about the behaviours of various gangs in our society. We see plenty of examples of this on American television where gangs based on ethnicity and social groupings form specific sets of behaviours that impact on how they interact with each other and the world. These groupings carry assumptions about how they see the world and respond to it. For example they have generally negative reactions to law enforcement and this is ingrained into their codes of behaviour. They are suspicious of the world and the people in it – dividing them up into threats, the law and victims. These behaviours are often reinforced by group experiences such as the initiation rituals which are integral to membership.

Often the impact of these behaviours is stereotypes that then categorise the individuals within these groups. The graphic I have included here shows a stereotypical gang member with the suspicious gaze, ubiquitous hoody and scruffy look. These stereotypes reject new ideas and maintain assumptions about the world, often to the detriment of their members. The experiences they have reinforce their own stereotypical way of viewing anything outside the safety of the group and the cycle continues. Of course, other groups have more positive impacts and see the world as a very different place and their experiences are designed to be positive interactions. Think about groups such as Rotary who are constructive in the community. Other groups have specialty interests such as Animal Welfare interests, Surf Lifesaving and charities.

List TWO groups that impact society through their behaviours. Try and develop one negative group and one positive group.

List some ways people can be influenced by belonging to a group.

Normal social interactions impact groups and individuals, but it takes a large scale event to alter the behaviours of societies, especially so in the modern world where societies are large scale. Earlier in human history smaller experiences could alter the behaviour of societies as they were insignificant in size to modern ones. We often fail to remember that many of these ancient societies' behaviours were impacted by superstition, religions and cultural habituation. The modern society as we know it is only a recent phenomenon. Just a few hundred years ago with church rule people were forced to think in a specific way and punished for not adhering to a theological culture. Think of the Spanish Inquisition, the imprisonment of Galileo and other such restrictions on freedom of thought and scientific breakthroughs were hidden or declared as witchcraft. Even recently the world has seen societies kept repressed by failed ideologies. The brutality of these regimes has left deep scars on the social psyche of nations as they try to recover. This has had an impact on the human experiences of whole populations, and societies respond accordingly.

One example might be at the conclusion of the Communist regime in East Germany when the Berlin Wall was symbolically destroyed as a visual symbol of the new-found freedom of a whole population of people who had been repressed for decades by a brutal and ever-present regime. Many citizens who had grown up in this system where you could 'disappear' without trial or real evidence found the idea that you could express yourself incredible. Many of the East Germans couldn't believe that this freedom was real and that the Stasi (secret police) were gone.

Other experiences can affect societies in extreme ways. Think about wars and the impact they have on civilian populations.

Climatic events such as earthquakes change the way that people behave and respond to situations. Catastrophic flooding occurred in the US city of New Orleans in 2005. The US President's response to help was not immediate and the national administration was severely criticised for lack of effective action.

Societies also respond to perceived problems such as pollution. In 1989 the oil tanker Exxon Valdez ran aground in Prince William Sound, Alaska with disastrous results (see the reports and images on the next page). The effects of this event are still being experienced thirty years later.

Societies can be divided, as we saw with the election of Donald Trump in the United States of America and the reaction of the left of politics.

The impact of human experiences on societies can be quite dramatic as we have seen, while other experiences (such as an election) can go by without a murmur from societies, whoever wins. As a last thought before we move on you should also consider the impact of the media on societies in the modern world, and how they influence individuals, societies and the development of ideas.

Exxon Valdez oil spill From Wikipedia, the free encyclopedia

The ***Exxon Valdez* oil spill** occurred in Prince William Sound, Alaska, March 24, 1989, when *Exxon Valdez*, an oil tanker owned by Exxon Shipping Company, bound for Long Beach, California, struck Prince William Sound's Bligh Reef at 12:04 am local time and spilled 10.8 million US gallons (260,000 bbl; 41,000 m^3) of crude oil over the next few days. It is considered to be one of the most devastating human-caused environmental disasters. The *Valdez* spill is the second largest in US waters, after the 2010 *Deepwater Horizon* oil spill, in terms of volume released. Prince William Sound's remote location, accessible only by helicopter, plane, or boat, made government and industry response efforts difficult and severely taxed existing response plans. The region is a habitat for salmon, sea otters, seals and seabirds. The oil, originally extracted at the Prudhoe Bay oil field, eventually covered 1,300 miles (2,100 km) of coastline, and 11,000 square miles (28,000 km^2) of ocean.

According to official reports, the ship was carrying 53.09451 million US gallons (1,264,155 bbl; 200,984.6 m^3) of oil, of which about 10.8 million US gallons (260,000 bbl; 41,000 m^3) were spilled into the Prince William Sound. An approximate figure of 11 million US gallons (260,000 bbl; 42,000 m^3) was a commonly accepted estimate of the spill's volume and has been used by the State of Alaska's *Exxon Valdez* Oil Spill Trustee Council, the National Oceanic and Atmospheric Administration and environmental groups such as Greenpeace and the Sierra Club

Workers using high-pressure, hot-water washing to clean an oiled shoreline

Shortly after leaving the Port of Valdez, the *Exxon Valdez* ran aground on Bligh Reef. The picture below was taken 3 days after the vessel grounded, just before a storm arrived.

During the first few days of the spill, heavy sheens of oil covered large areas of the surface of Prince William Sound.

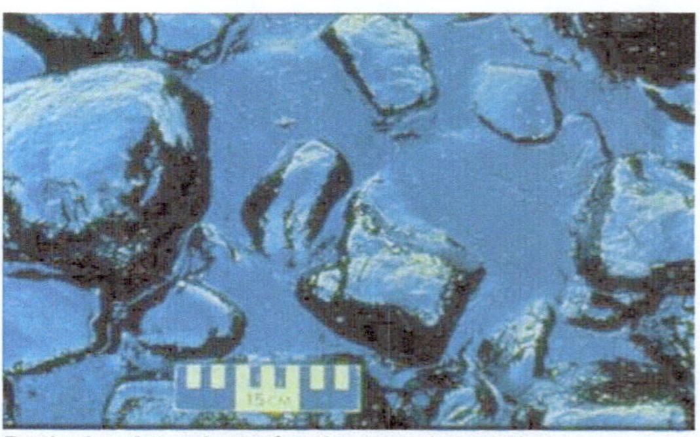

Beginning three days after the vessel grounded, a storm pushed large quantities of fresh oil on to the rocky shores of many of the beaches in the Knight Island chain. In this photograph, pooled black oil is shown stranded in the rocks

Wildlife was severely affected by the oil spill.

Decades later, on May 5, 2010, oil is shown seeping into a hole dug on a beach on Eleanor Island, Alaska

Give an example of an experience that has impacted and changed a society.

How do human experiences change the way we see the world and the assumptions and reflections we might make?

Think about your set text and consider one or more human experience(s) that impacts

1. **An individual**
2. **A group**
3. **A society**

Give a specific example and page reference. Explain your choice fully.

1.

2.

3.

What key ideas arise from these human experiences?

How does the text use language, form and structure to help create the experience for the reader?

Problems with Human Behaviour

So far we have discussed the impact of human experiences on behaviour. Now we can begin to make some more complex judgements and understandings about the impact of those experiences on human behaviours. In simplistic terms it could be assessed as:

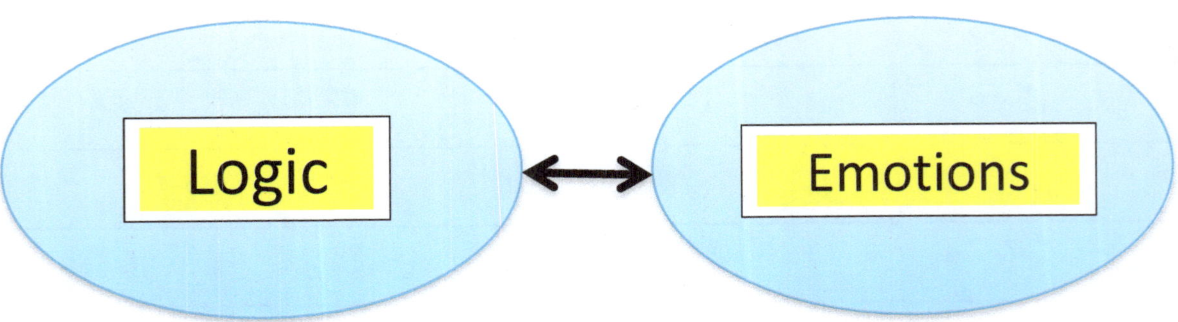

These two opposites on the continuum certainly move the manner in which we perceive incidents and how they affect our reaction. For instance, if someone you love has no interest in you it creates a very different reaction to someone you don't care about having no interest in you. It is generally agreed that humans respond more strongly with emotion than they do with logic. Often it is only through time and reflection that we can understand how an experience has changed and/or altered the manner in which we see a situation or individual.

The rubric points out that there are anomalies, inconsistencies and paradoxes in human behaviour and how people respond to experiences. You must keep this in mind when you examine your set text and search for related texts. Human experiences are responded to in a number of ways and it is often difficult to generalise, especially with individual experiences. Much of our response to experience is subjective and reactionary, not logical, especially without reflection. It is also significant to consider what individuals, groups and societies bring to the new experience. Prior experiences (learning) play a significant role in the response to an experience. Below are some questions to help you clarify these ideas. If you haven't completed the definitions of the three key words here (anomalies, inconsistencies and paradoxes) do that now.

In your own words define some problems with human behaviour(s).

When you think of the concept of emotions, what comes to mind?

Give an example of an emotional response to an experience you have had or witnessed. Why did you find it difficult to be logical?

Analysing a Scene – emotion vs logic

Carefully examine the picture below. In the space below assume the role of ONE of the characters and write how you are responding to the experience. It can be emotional or logical and if you can, write how the other person responds to your reaction to the same experience. Complete the task on your own paper.

The Role of Storytelling in Human Experiences

Storytelling has been part of the human experience since 'people' began communicating. It is a method used to convey information and experience and can also be entertaining. The earliest myths were all oral, and then people began to write down stories so they weren't lost in time. From this, various theories have developed around storytelling and one is the monomyth, which is a template across cultures for storytelling. Let's have a look at this below.

> In narratology and comparative mythology, the monomyth, or the hero's journey, is the common template of a broad category of tales that involve a hero who goes on an adventure, and in a decisive crisis wins a victory, and then comes home changed or transformed.
>
> The concept was introduced in *The Hero with a Thousand Faces* (1949) by Joseph Campbell, who described the basic narrative pattern as follows:
>
> > A hero ventures forth from the world of common day into a region of supernatural wonder: fabulous forces are there encountered and a decisive victory is won: the hero comes back from this mysterious adventure with the power to bestow boons on his fellow man.
>
> Campbell and other scholars, such as Erich Neumann, describe narratives of Gautama Buddha, Moses, and Christ in terms of the monomyth. Critics argue that the concept is too broad or general to be of much usefulness in comparative mythology. Others say that the hero's journey is only a part of the monomyth; the other part is a sort of different form, or colour, of the hero's journey.

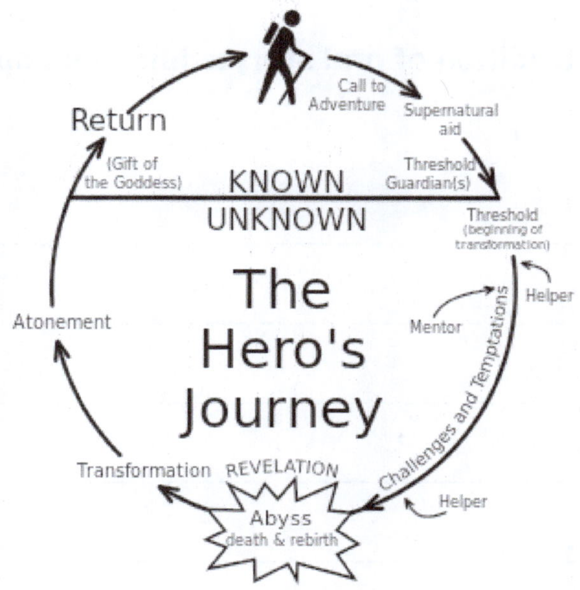

https://en.wikipedia.org/wiki/Hero%27s_journey

Describe the monomyth theory in your own words.

When you think of storytelling what comes to mind?

Why do you think a tradition of oral storytelling developed in all the human cultures?

Research one modern film/novel/short story etc. that fits into the monomyth theory. Why was this successful as a narrative?

Is there an element of the monomyth in your set text? If so give an example and page reference. Remember ONE element only need be present as not all texts will have the full pattern.

Storytelling in History and its Purpose in Human Experience

Storytelling in oral form was accompanied by some theatrics to make the stories as entertaining as possible. Many of the early narratives were based around religious ceremonies and stories of the creation of the earth and people(s). As time moved on these stories were accompanied by dance, music and/or theatre and often were part of lengthy rituals, often taking days. These stories were designed to bring meaning to people's lives by explaining their own existence and the purpose/meaning of life in a time when life expectancy was short and entertainment was scarce. Of course, stories were also recorded as these experiences were significant to all people, and these stories run across all cultures. Before writing, stories were recorded in pictures such as cave art, in tattoo designs on skin and in designs such as rock piles and the giant carved heads of Easter Island.

Writing changed the manner in which stories were told and some of the old oral traditions were lost, barely being kept alive by specialists. Stories began to transverse cultures and national boundaries on whatever surface could be created. Papyrus, bones, pottery, skins, paper and in more modern times film, video and digital storage have changed, over time, the way in which stories of the human experience have been told and shared. Content adapted from myth, fable and legend to history, personal narratives and commentary. Modern narrative form often has an educational or didactic content and can drift into propaganda. These stories of self-revelation can be instructive and give audiences the opportunity to apply learning to individual lives whereas historically narrative was used in this way for societies and groups. In recent times narratives have become interactive and audiences can choose how the narrative unfolds.

Whatever form the story takes we all have a seemingly innate need for narratives to make shape of our lives. They either confirm our world view or alter our world view depending on the experience they convey and the experiences that we bring to the narrative.

We need to remember that narratives are important to the human experience and have been significant since the beginning of time.

List some ways storytelling is conducted in the modern world. How might this influence the audience's perception of the story?

Give an example of a didactic form of narrative that you have experienced. Why do creators mask the 'message' behind the entertainment?

Give an example of this type of narrative form, conveying an idea in your set text.

The Text as an Experience

The concept of the text as an experience is one area to consider as we look at *Texts and Human Experience*. Reading or viewing the text is an experience in itself and when we do this we bring our own history (experiences) to the text and this helps shape our understanding.

Let's think about the personal perspective that we bring to a text. What are some of your experiences that might influence how you read a particular text? Some texts, especially personal narratives of trial and tribulation or loss, can be confronting to some audiences and bring back strong opinions or emotions. Many texts attempt to do this as they convey a particular point of view about the world.

Does what you bring to the text affect what you learn from that text? We also need to delve into how the narrative experience is conveyed and how this in turn impacts on the manner in which the story is received by audiences across different cultures. For example, Western films where heroes fight Islamic terrorism may well be viewed very differently by audiences in Western democracies and Islamic countries. Even seemingly innocuous narratives like the movie 'The Red Pill', which is about men's rights and was created by a woman has caused a polarisation of views wherever it has been shown. Strong personal experiences and viewpoints certainly bring their own understandings to texts.

In your own words list experiences that you have had that might influence how you read texts.

Universal themes are a noteworthy concept that creators use to keep audiences engaged in a narrative. Often they try to convey a particular impression of a universal theme or a viewpoint about the world using that theme. Universal themes can be considered in many ways shared experiences. They are things that affect us all such as love.

In your own words define what you understand a universal theme to be.

Analyse how universal themes enable connections to be made to a wide audience.

Afterword on Texts and Human Experience

Some human experiences will be happy and positive, fulfilling basic human needs and pushing us on to better things and more experiences. Other experiences will be negative and have deleterious effects on our existence. Texts transport all these experiences from real life situations to narrative experiences for us to judge their merit. Hopefully they challenge us and open up new ideas to our intellect and alter the manner in which we see the world and interact with it. Some texts may do this for one audience and not for others. A text may affect an individual significantly while having no impact whatsoever on another. There is no right or wrong answer. It is up to you to form your own opinions and come to conclusions about the text. Hopefully the material we have covered so far in this text will enable you to engage with texts and human experiences positively and with confidence so you won't experience what the two people below are feeling!

Unlock Your Ideas – In the space below draft out the introductory paragraphs to a speech for a teenage audience on texts and human experiences. Tell how a particular text impacted and changed a perception of a person, group or place. If you are ready to use your set text, do so!

WRITING TASKS – IMPROVING YOUR SKILLS

During your Year 12 studies you may be required to prepare a range of text types for different purposes. This section of the book seeks to give you some practical tips for improving your writing skills.

Organising your writing task response

Think about all the different forms of writing. With a few exceptions they all have a similar basic structure:

- A beginning
- A middle
- A conclusion

Certainly there are some specific variations based on the type of text. For example:

SHORT STORY

You have probably learnt what the text types structures for writing a narrative might involve:

- **Orientation**: who, what, why, where.
- **Complication**: something goes wrong, conflict
- **Resolution**: ending, does not have to be happy.

The Price of __________

While a poor woman stood in the marketplace selling cheeses, a cat came along and carried off a cheese. A dog saw the pilferer and tried to take the cheese away from him. The cat stood up to the dog. So they pitched into each other. The dog barked and snapped; the cat spat and scratched, but they could bring the battle to no decision.

"Let's go to the fox and have him referee the matter," the cat finally suggested.

"Agreed" said the dog. So they went to the fox. The fox listened to their arguments with a judicious air.

"Foolish animals," he chided them, "why carry on like that? If both of you are willing, I'll divide the cheese into two and you'll both be satisfied."

"Agreed," said the cat and the dog. So the fox took out his knife and cut the cheese in two, but, instead of cutting it lengthwise, he cut it in the width.

"My half is smaller!" protested the dog. The fox looked judiciously through his spectacles at the dog's share.

"You're quite right!" he decided. So he went and bit off a bit of the cat's share. "That will make it even!" he said. When the cat saw what the fox did she began to yowl: "Just look! My part's smaller now!" The fox again put on his spectacles and looked judiciously at the cat's share.

"Right you are!" said the fox.

"Just a moment and I'll make it right." And he went and bit a piece from the dog's cheese.

This went on so long, with the fox nibbling first at the dogs and then at the cats share, that he finally ate up the whole cheese before their eyes.

A Treasury of Jewish Folklore. Nathan Ausubel, Ed 1948

This parable, though short, has the basic elements of a piece of creative writing. There are **characters** and a **plot**, **time passing** and a place or **setting** is described. The theme binds the story together. But it is the reader who must interpret any meaning in the story. It is the questioning process in the reader's mind that makes the story. It is this thinking process in the reader's mind that makes the story enjoyable. This is the aim of the creative writer.

In our piece of writing, the characters are: ____________, ____________, ______________.

The plot (including the complication is):

____

____

____

____

Timeframe

____

____

Setting:

____

____

Theme

____

____

In an exam situation the examiner likes to see a clear complication not just lengthy description, although description is very important.

Plan your response to ONE of the following creative tasks. Ensure you present a perspective about human experience!

- *It was easy to feel isolated as nobody had found...*
- *Summertime anguish*
- *Puzzled she was*

Situation:

Complication:

Resolution:

Perspective on human experiences ?

Write the opening paragraph of your story.

Grabbing your audience

- The importance of an introduction
- The need for a "hook"
  - character focus
  - setting focus
  - a mystery/ the unknown
  - the short sentence

How do the following introductions attempt to grab the attention of the reader?

A lot of kids have nicknames. Like Mouse, or Bluey, or Freckles. Those sorts of nicknames are okay. My nickname was the Cow Dung Kid. Can you imagine that? The Cow Dung Kid. What a name to get stuck with.

The road dwindled into tracks that were little more than ruts gouged into yellow clay. They thinned and weakened to disappear finally in thick scrub, dank ferns and long grass. The place smelt of rotting vegetation, stale water and occasionally long-dead things. Even so, Norman dropped his bedroll and flopped on the ground. With his back propped against a tree he let his head loll to his chest to expose the fine skin that stretched over the nape of his neck. He slept, a lone boy in the bush.

This was the beginning of the end of my ordinary life.

Becca Dale sat on her own at the back of the class, staring out the window and hoping the hologram of Miss Young wouldn't scan around to where she was sitting.

How are hooks used in other forms of writing?

The Importance of Form

Form cannot be ignored!
Think about the different forms of writing that you do.

Any form has its own conventions of:

- Structure
- Paragraph use
- Sentence use
- Imagery use
- Person
- Tense

Select the form (e.g. short story) you are most confident with and discuss your strengths and weaknesses in it.

Select the form (e.g. poetry) you are weakest with and discuss your strengths and weaknesses in it.

Topic

In an exam situation you may be given a topic or stimulus material so you have a basis to begin with. Often it is a word or graphic that has some basis in a topic or you may have to make that link. In a more open class or personal choice situation the decision on what to write about can be quite difficult for the beginning writer. Here are some ideas:

- Feelings and experiences
- Media issues
- Textual issues
- Real life situations
- Social issues and problems
- Historical issues or reminiscences
- Your family
- Leisure, recreation and sports
- Personal problems or positive events
- Characters from the past or present

Circle the topics you think you have expertise in!

These are just a few ideas. If any of the items contained in the list above are unfamiliar to you I would suggest that you DO NOT write about them as it is best to be good at the familiar and then expand on your repertoire. For example, if you know nothing about computers or any of the jargon, do not write about them. However, if you have spent your life in front of a monitor it may be a good proposition. Many students like science fiction as they think they can make it up. Don't fall into this trap. Remember to link the material you are using to the stimulus material and think about what aspect of the human experience you are conveying.

The secret of success in creative writing is to write regularly and give your writing time priority.

What are some topics in the common module you might be able to write about?

____

____

____

____

Audience

When you write it is always for an audience, even if that audience is just you! It is important to keep your audience in mind when you write as it will affect both your topic and vocabulary. For example it is no use writing a technical, jargon encrusted journal article for an audience of pre-school children.

Some examples of audience are:

- Examiners/teachers
- Children
- Teenagers
- Adults
- General public
- Your peer group
- Specific audiences such as brain surgeons, rocket scientists
- Technical journals
- Blogs for specific groups such as coin collectors

Always remember that you are writing for an audience – even if it is personal writing meant only for you. The audience are the 'judges' of your work and if their needs are not met they won't read on. You need to be engaging and have the appropriate language and content to keep them reading!

Who is your audience in Paper One of the HSC? This is a very important question. What we are really asking is who is marking your work?

How might this affect what you write and how you write it?

Purpose

Once you have an idea of what you are going to write and who you are writing for, you are in a position to determine the purpose of your writing. Some pieces of writing entertain, others inform or instruct. Written texts have also been used as propaganda. A good piece of writing will stimulate reflection and provoke some type of response from the reader.

The best thing about a writing task is that it can be as simple or complex as you choose it to be. It can be a simple communication like the story at the beginning of the lecture to prove a point or it can be written with ironic or satiric complexity. Whatever you write it will be better if it has a purpose and can make some kind of point or reveal something about the human experience. An easy way to have a purpose is to include as an idea one of the universal themes – just like Shakespeare did.

Some writing hints

Below we have listed some ideas from our experience as educators on how to make the most with your writing.

- PLAN PLAN PLAN! You must not dive in and realise by the second page you have no idea what you are writing about. Your response must go somewhere. Decide this before you begin.
- Consider rejecting the first two ideas that come to you – they could be the ones everyone else has thought of too!
- Use what you have learnt to begin a response immediately. Too much wasted exam time will leave you short in the other sections.
- Try and make your introductory paragraph have impact.
- Focus on the purpose of the piece. Create the idea that the writing is going somewhere, even in paragraphs and sentences. Actions have consequences, or ought to. Every sentence included in a writing piece should be necessary to it.
- Use detail in description, but avoid the boring and mundane details unless you have a good reason to use them.
- Use direct speech by all means but avoid the tedium of *he said/ she said* and be very careful with the punctuation.
- Short sentences are generally better than those that ramble.

- Do not try and compact a novel into a short piece. This loses the detail that you need.

- If the form allows it, use some of the literary techniques that you have been taught and studied at school such as symbols, imagery, alliteration, repetition, similes, etc.
- Check the punctuation, paragraphs, sentences, spelling and tense. These are simple things where candidates often fall down. Practise editing every time you write.

- In creative pieces, do not just focus on plot. Include all or some of the things we have discussed today. But also don't dwell too much on the scenery or setting unless it illuminates or motivates a character.

- Avoid the use of clichés unless they are directly relevant and part of your purpose.

- Avoid writing about offensive themes or actions. Most examiners would also recommend avoiding poetry and maintain that good humour is very difficult to write.

- Never write about your experience with the HSC, your emotional angst with your girlfriend/boyfriend, your schoolies week planned exploits, how you hate school/life/everything.

- Only try for the 'twist' ending if it is appropriate and you can think of one!

- Above all answer the question and/or respond to the stimulus material that is supplied. Do not go off on a tangent or try to use a prepared response.

What TWO tips do you think will help you most?

TIP ONE

____

____

____

____

TIP TWO

____

____

____

____

Drafting and Editing

In a non-exam situation the following hints are useful to improve your writing to prepare you for the pressure of writing in an exam or to meet a deadline.

- You should write one draft and leave it for a while. This means you can't leave things until the last minute.Check the draft for:
    - *spelling errors*
    - *punctuation*
    - *sustained development of ideas*
    - *effective communication*
    - *language*
    - *audience*
    - *vocabulary*
    - *form/structure*
    - *paragraphing*
    - *interest level*
    - *meeting the requirements of the question or stimulus*

- The introduction and conclusion should be of particular importance.

- Re-work the draft and edit the orientation where necessary. At this point vocabulary can be corrected and improved, perhaps with a thesaurus. Nowadays it is easy with the thesaurus in Word or an on-line version. Just make sure it makes sense and you aren't just using high level vocabulary for the sake of it.

- Try and show someone your work. It can be either a peer or a trusted adult. Ask them for an opinion but remind them that it is a draft and not to be over critical. Ask for THREE things to fix or else they will just tell you it's 'wonderful'.

- If you have time, write a re-draft and go through the process again. This may seem repetitive but, as with everything, practice is important. The more you practise these techniques the better your work will become and the easier it will be to do.

Descriptive Writing Activities

Description is essential to any piece of creative writing and part of the flair of many other forms like articles or journals. It is through effective description that your reader is immersed into the world you create. Description often uses:

- Adjectives
- Similes
- Metaphors
- Personification

Quality description avoids worn adjectives and images: clichés are too dull to stimulate the imagination. You need to work on creating images that are your own. Avoid descriptions you have heard many times before.

ACTIVITY – Eliminating Clichés

Here are some really stale, worn out descriptions. Change each of them to something fresh and imaginative!

For example *I had butterflies in my stomach* would be far fresher if it was something more original like *I had a feisty rhinoceros butting my insides.*

(a) It was a hot and sunny day.

(b) The girl had beautiful blonde hair.

(c) Shivers ran up my spine.

(d) It was an old, creepy house.

ACTIVITY – Improving our vocabulary

One thing that will really make a difference to your writing is widening your vocabulary. Often we know words but we don't think to use them. We need to expand our working vocabulary so we can explain exactly what we mean.

> Don't go overboard. You only need a few good words to lift a piece. Experiment but don't overdo it. This can sound ridiculous and impede your effect.

Here are two lists of words. The first column has words students commonly use in writing tasks. The second column has words you probably know but may not use. Match up each with what it means and then use each of the more imaginative, second column words in a sentence.

Column One	Column Two
kind	ecstatic
happy	soothe
sad	malevolent
beautiful	envisage
dull	morose
hardworking	benevolent
unclear	drab
short	succinct
see	diligent
calm	alluring
evil	ambiguous

Now can you choose TWO words from Column Two to use in a sentence?

1

____

____

____

2

____

____

____

ACTIVITY – Varying our sentences

A piece of writing can also be made more interesting and descriptive by varying the types of sentences we use. A sophisticated writer does not repeatedly begin their sentences with *He (She, It ...)* or *The* but instead varies the types of words they use. They might use

- Adverbs (eg. 'ly' words)
- Participles (e.g. 'ing' words)
- Nouns
- Adjectives

Again, don't go overboard but be aware of the technique.

Use the following to start sentences with:

Adverbs

(a) Sadly

(b) Contentedly

Participles

(a) Leaping

(b) Spinning

Nouns

(a) Laughter

(b) Mischief

Adjectives

(a) Immense

(b) Towering

ACTIVITY – A descriptive paragraph

Use the above activities to change the following, very dull, paragraph into something far more creative. Feel free to add detail!

It was a beautiful summer's day. The big dog ran across the road. Its coat was as black as night. It was hungry and thirsty.

A Writing Task

Using ONE of the following images as a stimulus, compose a piece of imaginative writing that explores human experiences. The stimulus must be an integral part of your writing.

Think about the types of human experiences we discussed at the beginning of this book if you are struggling to think of ideas.

However feel free to write about any type of experience you can think about — the more creative the better!

Using ONE of the following quotes somewhere in a creative response:

Hint: remember to keep the focus on human experiences

The world sometimes feels like an insane asylum. You can decide whether you want to be an inmate or pick up your visitor's badge. You can be in the world but not engage in the melodrama of it; you can become a spiritual being having a human experience thoroughly and fully.

Deepak Chopra

OR

'There are some experiences you just don't want to have!'

OR

I think what's important is to give space to the range of human experience.

Judy Chicago

Construct an imaginative writing piece about a type of experience of your own choosing. Attempt to write about a different experience than your first writing piece. You can begin below and then finish on your own paper.

ADVANCED, STANDARD AND ENGLISH STUDIES: COMMON MODULE

'THE SHORT ANSWERS' – Paper One Section One

General Tips and Ideas

The key before you begin is to think about:

WHAT and HOW questions: *what's* being said... and *how* it is represented (techniques)

- ***Read before you start***

Read the texts (10 minutes reading time helps)

Read the questions – Check you don't answer the next part. Know exactly what you are asked in each part.

- ***Allocated marks are important***

Marks awarded indicate how long you should spend on an answer.

These are only general guides. It is not Maths so do not follow any guidelines too exactly. Do what you have to do to answer the question!

1 mark: probably only a sentence or two. Not paragraphs!
2 marks: a paragraph
3 marks: two or three paragraphs
4 marks: three or four paragraphs
5 marks: Three or more exam booklet pages

- ***Know your language techniques***

Different forms use different techniques. Here are some common language techniques:

COMMON PROSE TECHNIQUES

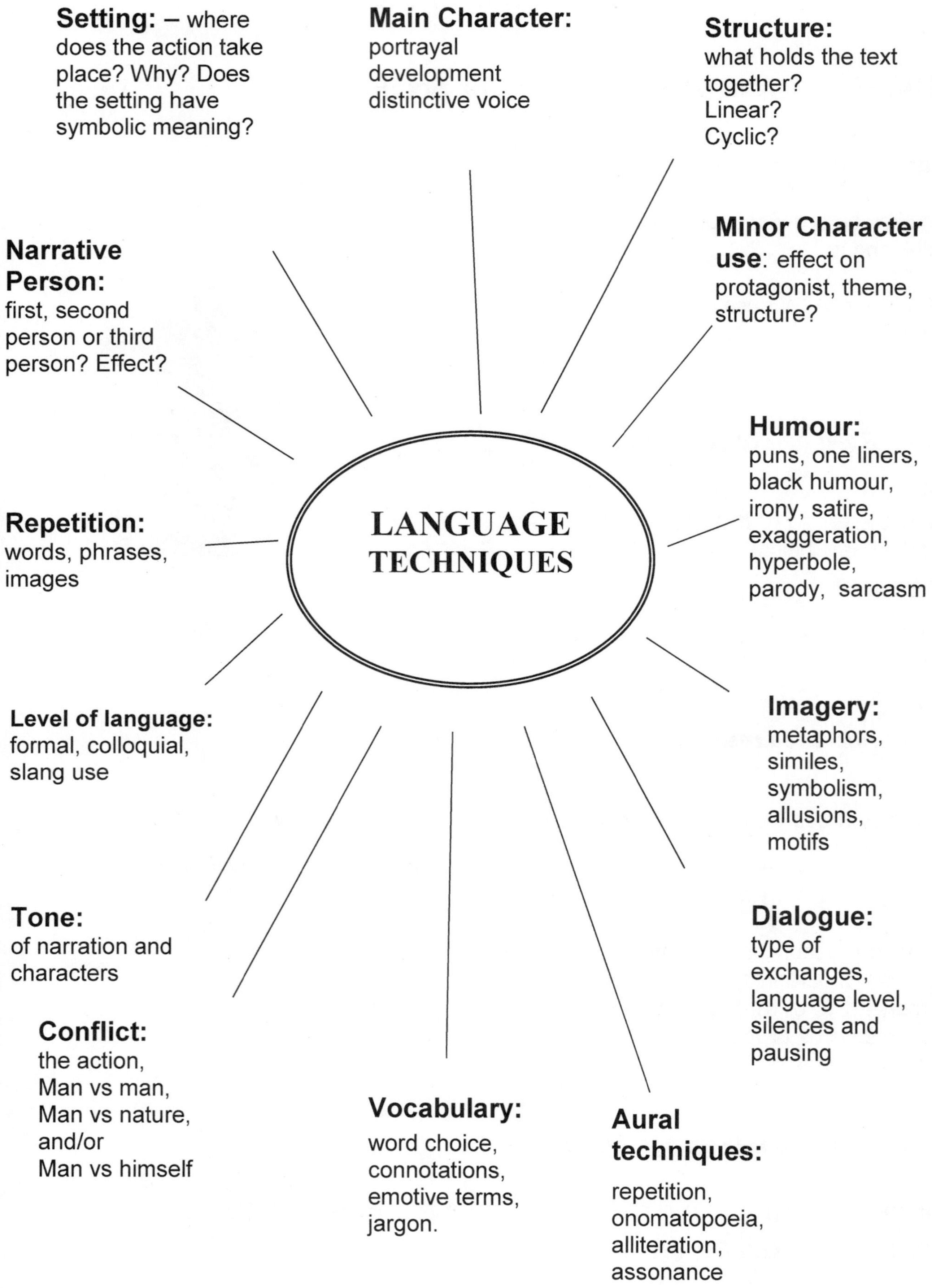

LANGUAGE TECHNIQUES

Setting: – where does the action take place? Why? Does the setting have symbolic meaning?

Main Character: portrayal development distinctive voice

Structure: what holds the text together? Linear? Cyclic?

Narrative Person: first, second person or third person? Effect?

Minor Character use: effect on protagonist, theme, structure?

Humour: puns, one liners, black humour, irony, satire, exaggeration, hyperbole, parody, sarcasm

Repetition: words, phrases, images

Level of language: formal, colloquial, slang use

Imagery: metaphors, similes, symbolism, allusions, motifs

Tone: of narration and characters

Dialogue: type of exchanges, language level, silences and pausing

Conflict: the action, Man vs man, Man vs nature, and/or Man vs himself

Vocabulary: word choice, connotations, emotive terms, jargon.

Aural techniques: repetition, onomatopoeia, alliteration, assonance

Know your visual techniques

When analysing a visual text, which can include a photograph, advertisement, cartoon, drawing, poster etc. we must look at the visual techniques it uses to establish meaning. Look at the listed visual techniques and ask yourself the following questions when you analyse a visual text. These will help you draw as much meaning as possible from these texts and will allow you to be able to analyse it on a deeper and more sound level. Keep in mind that language techniques can sometimes work hand in hand with the visual techniques.

- **Body Language** – the stance, gestures, facial expressions and position of our subject. The way someone is standing and how they are holding their body can say a lot about how they are feeling or their attitude towards something.

- **Costume** – what is the subject/s wearing? This can say a lot about a person. Note the colour and style of the costumes and what that can represent about a person, place, time or thing.

- **Colour and Tone** - think about certain colour palettes, what do neon, vibrant colours tell us opposed to dark and dreary colours? Think about colours representing certain emotions and feelings. For example: red representing love, passion or anger and green representing envy, money or nature etc.

- **Contrast** – creating tension or emotion through the placing of opposite elements i.e. good vs evil, light vs dark, rich vs poor, long vs short etc.

- **Framing** – think about the camera angles we look at when analysing a film - the same applies with visual texts: close up, extreme close up, long shot, mid shot, low angle shot, high angle shot, birds-eye view etc. What is the purpose in the way the image has been framed? What does this tell us?

- **<u>Gaze</u>** – the eye line of a subject. Think about where they are looking? Or what they are looking at?

- **<u>Juxtaposition</u>** – when two objects or subjects have been placed next or near each other to show difference.

- **<u>Modality</u>** – if an image is high in modality then it could be considered 'realistic' or 'truthful' - an example would be a high definition photograph. However, if an image is low in modality then it doesn't resemble something in a realistic way, an example could be a cartoon drawing of someone or an abstract image that represents something else.

- **<u>Montage/Collage</u>** – a cluster of different images that make up a larger image. Used usually to allow more content to be displayed or for stylistic purposes.

- **<u>Omissions</u>** – what has been deliberately left out?

- **<u>Positioning</u>** – how have the subjects and other objects been placed? Are they in the background, in the middle or at the front? What does this say?

- **<u>Salience</u>** – what is the part of the image that your eyes are most drawn to? Usually a colour or subject, but can be something else, this is referred to as the salient image.

- **<u>Surroundings</u>** – what objects make up the less dominant parts of the image? What can these tell us about the location or other details about the image?

- **<u>Symbolism</u>** – the use of an image or object to represent a theme or a more complex idea. Some examples could include a rose symbolising love or a clock symbolising time.

- **<u>Vectors</u>** – these are the lines our eyes make when looking at visual texts. It may be the gaze of a subject that has forced its viewer to focus on whatever the subject is looking at, or it could possibly be the line of a pathway or road that has been designed for the viewer to follow this line and direct their attention to where it's leading.

Discovering With Your Eyes!

Have a look at the image below. Let's take a closer look at it and begin to analyse it further using the language we have just read.

Comment on the following and how this image explores the human experience through the listed visual techniques:

- Body language, positioning and costume of the subject(s)

- Framing of the image

- The subject's (choose one) gaze and vectors

- The salience and modality

- The colour palette

- Symbolism and surroundings

What does this text show/explain/offer about human experiences?

Know the terms used in questions

Use the table below to research and define the terms in your own words. State also how you might approach a question that includes that word.

Identify	
Explain	
Analyse	
Describe	
Compare	

Below are some text types that you may find in Paper One of the HSC.

Analyse the texts and answer the questions that follow.

Image

How does this image convey a sense of human experience(s)?

Poems

The following two poems show contrasting human experiences. They come from the poetry of William Blake and have the title *Songs of Innocence and Experience*. The poems show us the innocence of the little boy and his desire to be loved while the second poem shows the experience of the young sweep and the realities of his life. Read the poems carefully and answer the questions that follow.

THE LITTLE BLACK BOY

My mother bore me in the southern wild,
And I am black, but oh my soul is white!
White as an angel is the English child,
But I am black, as if bereaved of light.

My mother taught me underneath a tree,
And, sitting down before the heat of day,
She took me on her lap and kissed me,
And, pointed to the east, began to say:

"Look on the rising sun: there God does live,
And gives His light, and gives His heat away,
And flowers and trees and beasts and men receive
Comfort in morning, joy in the noonday."

"And we are put on earth a little space,
That we may learn to bear the beams of love
And these black bodies and this sunburnt face
Is but a cloud, and like a shady grove."

"For when our souls have learn'd the heat to bear,
The cloud will vanish, we shall hear His voice,
Saying, 'Come out from the grove, my love and care
And round my golden tent like lambs rejoice',"

'Thus did my mother say, and kissed me;
And thus I say to little English boy.
When I from black and he from white cloud free,
And round the tent of God like lambs we joy

I'll shade him from the heat till he can bear
To lean in joy upon our Father's knee;
And then I'll stand and stroke his silver hair,
And be like him, and he will then love me.

THE CHIMNEY SWEEPER

A little black thing in the snow,
Crying "weep! weep!" in notes of woe!
"Where are thy father and mother? Say!"—
"They are both gone up to the church to pray.

"Because I was happy upon the heath,
And smiled among the winter's snow,
They clothed me in the clothes of death,
And taught me to sing the notes of woe.

"And because I am happy and dance and sing,
They think they have done me no injury,
And are gone to praise God and his priest and king,
Who make up a heaven of our misery."

Discuss ONE poem in terms of human experience and state what purpose the poem has.

____

____

____

____

____

____

____

What is Blake saying about human experience with the title S*ongs of Innocence and Experience*?

____

____

____

____

____

Speech Extract

The following is the full speech by American President Ronald Reagan which speaks to the American people about the January 28 1986 accident that killed seven Americans including the first civilian astronaut, Christa McAuliffe. The accident occurred just 73 seconds into the flight and it shocked the nation. This is rated as one of the great speeches of all time and it shows different aspects of the human experience.

Ladies and Gentlemen, I'd planned to speak to you tonight to report on the state of the Union, but the events of earlier today have led me to change those plans. Today is a day for mourning and remembering. Nancy and I are pained to the core by the tragedy of the shuttle Challenger. We know we share this pain with all of the people of our country. This is truly a national loss.

Nineteen years ago, almost to the day, we lost three astronauts in a terrible accident on the ground. But, we've never lost an astronaut in flight; we've never had a tragedy like this. And perhaps we've forgotten the courage it took for the crew of the shuttle; but they, the Challenger Seven, were aware of the dangers, but overcame them and did their jobs brilliantly. We mourn seven heroes: Michael Smith, Dick Scobee, Judith Resnik, Ronald McNair, Ellison Onizuka, Gregory Jarvis, and Christa McAuliffe. We mourn their loss as a nation together.

For the families of the seven, we cannot bear, as you do, the full impact of this tragedy. But we feel the loss, and we're thinking about you so very much. Your loved ones were daring and brave, and they had that special grace, that special spirit that says, 'Give me a challenge and I'll meet it with joy.' They had a hunger to explore the universe and discover its truths. They wished to serve, and they did. They served all of us.

We've grown used to wonders in this century. It's hard to dazzle us. But for twenty-five years the United States space program has been doing just that. We've grown used to the idea of space, and perhaps we forget that we've only just begun. We're still pioneers. They, the members of the Challenger crew, were pioneers.

And I want to say something to the schoolchildren of America who were watching the live coverage of the shuttle's takeoff. I know it is hard to understand, but sometimes painful things like this happen. It's all part of the process of exploration and discovery. It's all part of taking a chance and expanding man's horizons. The future doesn't belong to the fainthearted; it belongs to the brave. The Challenger crew was pulling us into the future, and we'll continue to follow them.

I've always had great faith in and respect for our space program, and what happened today does nothing to diminish it. We don't hide our space program. We don't keep secrets and cover things up. We do it all up front and in public. That's the way freedom is, and we wouldn't change it for a minute. We'll continue our quest in space. There will be more shuttle flights and more shuttle crews and, yes, more volunteers, more civilians, more teachers in space. Nothing ends here; our hopes and our journeys continue. I want to add that I wish I could talk to every man and woman who works for NASA or who worked on this mission and tell them: "Your dedication and professionalism have moved and impressed us for decades. And we know of your anguish. We share it."

There's a coincidence today. On this day 390 years ago, the great explorer Sir Francis Drake died aboard ship off the coast of Panama. In his lifetime the great frontiers were the oceans, and a historian later said, 'He lived by the sea, died on it, and was buried in it.' Well, today we can say of the Challenger crew: Their dedication was, like Drake's, complete.

The crew of the space shuttle Challenger honoured us by the manner in which they lived their lives. We will never forget them, nor the last time we saw them, this morning, as they prepared for the journey and waved goodbye and 'slipped the surly bonds of earth' to 'touch the face of God.'

Thank you.

Explain how Reagan accepts loss as part of the human experience and reassures the American people.

Discuss the lines below in terms of human experience.

"It's all part of taking a chance and expanding man's horizons. The future doesn't belong to the fainthearted; it belongs to the brave. The Challenger crew was pulling us into the future, and we'll continue to follow them."

Discuss how Reagan shows this sense of needing to experience is part of the human psyche. You may use the quote from the speech below to help in your response.

"There's a coincidence today. On this day 390 years ago, the great explorer Sir Francis Drake died aboard ship off the coast of Panama. In his lifetime the great frontiers were the oceans, and a historian later said, 'He lived by the sea, died on it, and was buried in it.' Well, today we can say of the Challenger crew: Their dedication was, like Drake's, complete."

Prose Fiction

The extract below is from Charles Dickens' novel *A Tale of Two Cities*. It shows the paradoxes and confusions in human existence and succinctly analyses the world. It is one of the most famous passages in literature and is often quoted in reference to how the world is perceived.

> **'It was the best of times, it was the worst of times, it was the age of wisdom, it was the age of foolishness, it was the epoch of belief, it was the epoch of incredulity, it was the season of Light, it was the season of Darkness, it was the spring of hope, it was the winter of despair, we had everything before us, we had nothing before us, we were all going direct to Heaven, we were all going direct the other way – in short, the period was so far like the present period, that some of its noisiest authorities insisted on its being received, for good or for evil, in the superlative degree of comparison only.'**

What is Dickens saying about human experience here?

____

____

____

____

____

____

How does Dickens express his ideas about the human experience in this short text?

____

____

____

____

Do you agree with Dickens' interpretation about the contrasts in perception about human experiences? You may draw on ONE other text to support your ideas if you wish.

What TWO texts would you choose to add in a document that provides examples of human experiences for HSC students?

Explain the reasons for your choices and make specific references to the texts.

Text One

Text Two

THE SUSTAINED RESPONSE – Paper One Section Two

In the English HSC Paper One there will be one question in Section II. The question will require a sustained response based on the candidate's prescribed text. The question may include stimulus and/or unseen texts.

REMEMBER TO LINK YOUR RESPONSE TO THE HUMAN EXPERIENCE AS INSTRUCTED!

NESA has mandated that students must study a related text as part of the common module, and that this should be part of their in-school assessment. However there is **no longer** a requirement to write about a related text in the HSC examination itself.

- ***Understand the module: Texts and Human Experiences***

Just a quick refresher to ensure understanding. What are "human experiences"?

List FIVE things you have learned about human experiences

1

2

3

4

5

Answer the question – Have a thesis!

Don't just retell texts. Have an argument and make sure you can support it with evidence from the text(s) you have studied. Remember you must refer to the specific text chosen by your teacher for this common module and you may have to respond to an unseen stimulus and/or unseen text. Your argument (thesis) should be able to be supported with this evidence and be consistent throughout the sustained response.

e.g. What is your line of argument for the following question? Don't just agree, say WHY!

The WHY is the most important bit!

- ***Know your prescribed text well***

✓ Know what happens

✓ Decide what it says about Human Experiences

✓ Have quotes and incidents as evidence

✓ Use specific quotes and examples to support your idea

✓ Human experiences are about many things such as ideas, emotions and personal responses so don't limit yourself but remember to support each idea with adequate evidence.

✓ For higher standard responses focus on language techniques, but don't just list the technique(s), state why the creator has used that technique. The best answers also reflect the impact of that technique on the audience.

✓ Three or four well developed ideas are better than many unsubstantiated thoughts. Structure these points around your original thesis.

Practise planning and writing responses

'Story-telling provides an insight into ourselves and shared human experiences.'

To what extent have you seen this in your study of Texts and Human Experiences? In your response refer to your prescribed text.

THESIS: Main Points:

Sample Texts to Develop Ideas

Jasper Jones by Craig Silvey

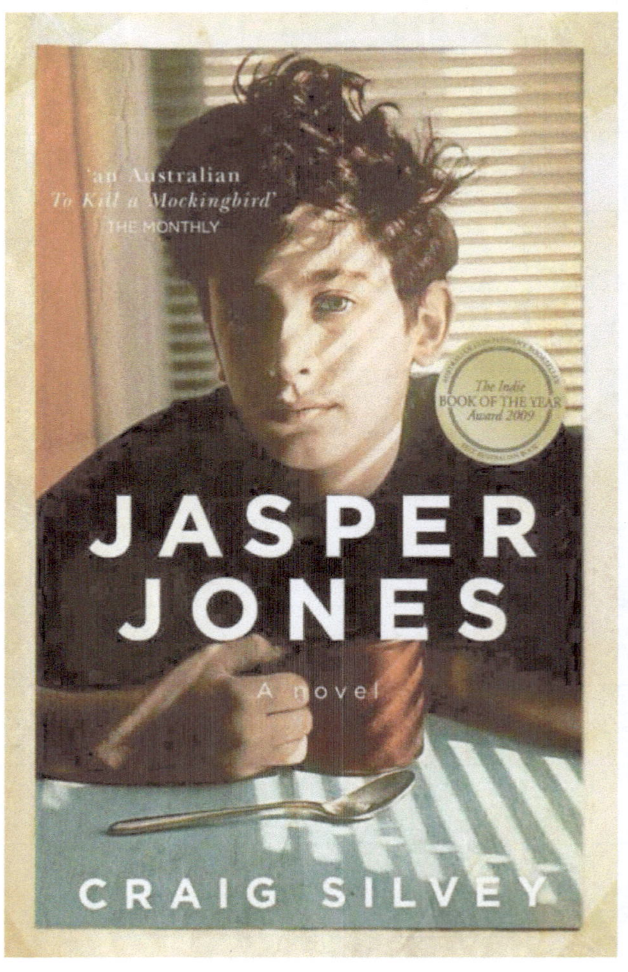

Set in the 1960s in a regional mining town in Western Australia, on a hot summer's night 13 year old Charlie and the rebellious town outcast Jasper Jones come across a gruesome and horrible discovery. This sets off a chain of experiences that will change the boys' lives forever. It is a book that explores how hard experiences can sometimes lead to enlightening truths about us, others and the world around us. The novel urges its characters and the audience to open their eyes to the world and the harsh realities that can exist in that world. It clarifies the idea that experiences can be life changing and that we should always learn from our experiences.

To Kill a Mockingbird by Harper Lee (1960)

This is a brilliant expose of the American south and the actions of lawyer and father Atticus Finch in a world of racism and bigotry. One man's experiences and beliefs that are shaped by those experiences are central to a novel that shows how implacable some experiences make people and how difficult it is to create change. There is a lot in this novel that could be drawn out for this Common Module.

Room by Emma Donoghue (2010)

Room is told from the perspective of five year old Jack, who has been held captive in a room with his mother for his entire life. One day Jack's mother sets up a plan to free both of them and when it surprisingly works, Jack has to learn to live in the real world which is scary and unfamiliar to him. A book which explores the concept of how a lack of experiences lead to a new world and learning to adapt, readjust and survive within an unfamiliar place. It is an interesting look at how minimalist experiences and interactions shape a character and a life.

The Giver by Lois Lowry (1993)

A novel set in a dystopian future where everything and everyone is perfect, there is no war, hate, hunger or suffering. Our protagonist Jonas soon discovers that things such as love, choice, independence and adventure were sacrificed in order for this seemingly perfect existence. Jonas has many experiences during this book that makes him constantly question his world and comes to the realisation that without risk, danger and self-control, you are not really living.

Non-fiction

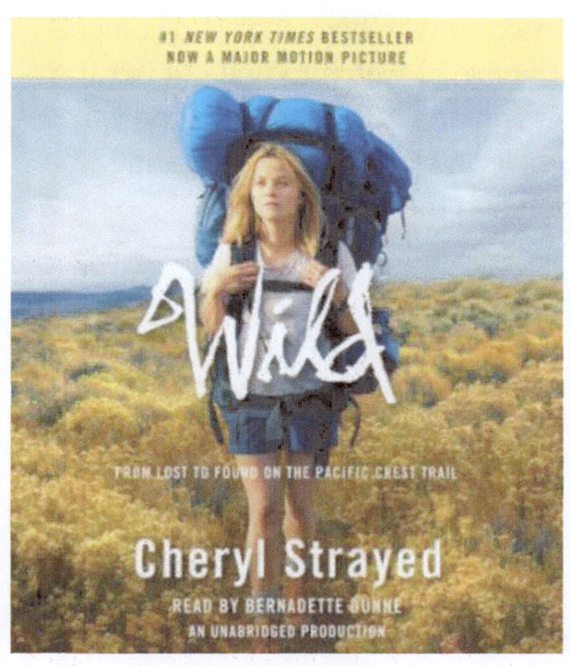

Wild: From Lost to Found on the Pacific Crest Trail by Cheryl Strayed (2012)

A first-person memoir, from a woman named Cheryl Strayed who undertook a 1,100 mile hike along the Pacific Crest Trail in the USA, an amazing experience. The book also contains flashbacks to Strayed's experiences in life prior to the hike. Battling grief and drug abuse, Strayed embarks on this hike, with no prior experience, and beings a journey of self-discovery enduring physical obstacles and spiritual realisations because of the experiences she is subjected to. This book (and film version) also encourages its readers to go outdoors and experience life for themselves to see how healing and therapeutic the natural world can be. This text highlights a major positive transformation due to a host of experiences and is both publicly and critically acclaimed.

Fat, Sick and Nearly Dead by Joe Cross and Kurt Engfher (2010)

This documentary tracks the story of Joe Cross as he begins his own journey to health and exposes his own personal health journey. He is 310lb man who commits to a personal journey to regain his health and inspire others along the way. He takes a road trip in America to meet others with the same problems. He does this and the main focus becomes Phil Staples, a truckie who is even closer to his final burger. The documentary covers their experiences from overweight to healthy and what this new perspective brings to their lives and future experiences. This is a clearly engaging film and the Australian connection should also resonate with viewers. We get a few very different experiences around health and life in general, including how the characters are perceived by others. It is interesting to note that the experiences shared in the documentary have inspired others to follow suit and take up the juice diet and healthy lifestyle.

The King of Kong: A Fistful of Quarters by Seth Gordon (2007)

This documentary examines the obsessive world of gaming but in a retrospective kind of way with classic arcade games and the record holders. To us it might just be a game but to these people it is life. Go back to the early 80s when the 'legend' Billy Mitchell set a Donkey Kong record. After twenty five years Steve Wiebe breaks that record under supervision at 'Funspot' and Mitchell retaliates by sending in a controversial tape of himself breaking the new record. Will they meet and compete live and settle the matter once and for all? You'll have to watch to find out but the human experience here is about complete obsession and how that alters the way you see and experience the world and other people. A highly rated fascinating documentary that tells us a lot about competition and the world through experiencing a small microcosm of it.

Drama

Death of a Salesman by Arthur Miller (1949)

Death of a Salesman was first performed in 1949 in London. This is just a few years after the end of the Second World War. It is a period of history that we associate with prosperity and optimism in America. Miller turns his attention to this period immediately after the war, characterised by opportunity, ambition and optimism. It is especially this optimism that he questions – what are the dreams of humanity in this situation and how do these dreams compare to reality? The play tries to get the audience into Willy Loman's mind – the set is a representation of Willy's mind and it visually captures for the audience the relationship between the past and the present. Willy's experiences become divorced from reality and the expectations of those around him become shaped by what he does and says until the truth is revealed. Willy represents the experiences of many which are in conflict with the opportunities and hopes of the time, his success is mythical and the dream is the experience.

Film

Memento directed by Christopher Nolan (2000)

Leonard Shelby is a man suffering. He suffers in his search for revenge against the man who raped and murdered his wife. He also suffers from a rare, untreatable form of memory loss where he can't remember anything short term but has details from his more distant past. He uses photos, tattoos and notes etc. to keep track of his experiences so that he can maintain his quest for revenge. Memento is an amazing film about one unique human experience. It is an original film that still utilises all the hallmarks of a thriller. Critically acclaimed and an enthralling watch.

Gattaca directed by Andrew Niccol (1999)

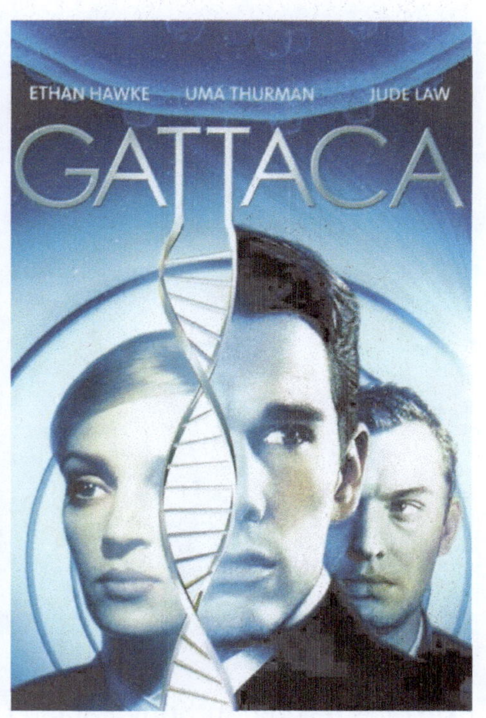

Imagine being imperfect in a world that is designed for genetic perfection. This is the problem for Vincent who is genetically 'In-Valid' and who seeks to pursue his ultimate goal of travelling into space as an astronaut for the Gattaca Aerospace Corporation. He assumes the identity of a genetically perfect man, using samples from him to assist him to pass all the tests required to fly. Shortly before he is to fly and fulfil his goal a murder is committed and he becomes a suspect, throwing his carefully laid plans awry. He is pursued by the detective in charge of the case and as the pressure is applied he also is doubted by the woman he has fallen in love with. A great science fiction film with the focus of the human experience that is common to us all despite our differences.

Little Miss Sunshine directed by Valerie Faris and Jonathan Dayton (2006)

When 7 year old Olive learns that she has qualified for a beauty pageant competition in California, a dysfunctional family set off on a road trip to get her there. As we follow this family's experiences on the road, each family member goes through the process of various experiences, each pursuing something or working through an issue. A film about how experiences never quite go to plan and the dreams and aspirations that we think we want can sometimes be the wrong things for us. We witness this family rediscover one another and learn new things about each other on the way.

The Breakfast Club directed by John Hughes (1985)

It's Saturday and five very different students have detention with one another, there's a jock, a princess, a nerd, a misfit and a rebel. With such diverse backgrounds, differing life experiences and nothing in common a lot of friction and tension ensues. However, once they begin to talk and get to know one another they discover they have a lot more in common than they think through the common experiences they have, especially as teenagers navigating the complexities of an adult world. Over the day the students learn more about themselves and their new friends once they learnt to give each other a chance and opened themselves up to new experiences and ideas. One of the great teen flicks from this period and these shared experiences set in a tight narrative form are ideal for study.

Skin directed by Anthony Fabian (2010)

A true story set in South Africa in the time of apartheid. The human experiences this text shares with the audience are unusual to say the least but the theme of human dignity and love shine through. Sandra Laing was a black child born in the 1950s to two Afrikaner parents unaware of their black heritage. Until the age of ten Sandra was treated as a white in the local community where her parents ran the local shop. After this she had to navigate, with her parents, the complex and convoluted race laws that deemed people white, coloured or black. It takes thirty years and a lot of heartache and court appearances before Sandra can reconcile with who she is. Her experience in a world where race is at the core of existence is a journey where she has to negotiate her own experiences with those of others whose experiences have them set against her.

Brokeback Mountain directed by Ang Lee (2005)

A powerful film about two young men. They meet and experience sexual attraction towards one another in the summer of 1963, whilst sheep-herding on a mountain in Wyoming. What follows is a love story about experiencing your own sexuality and coming to terms with it in a society that rejects that experience and can react violently to it. The two men live in a society that does not accept who they really are and they begin to live in fear of people discovering their relationship. The film then follows the men over the next few decades as we witness these men experience the world, themselves, and what it means to be gay in a hostile environment. The human experiences in this text illustrate how experiences shape lives and attitudes even if they are not social norms.

Jindabyne directed by Ray Lawrence (2006)

When three men go on a fishing trip into the isolated Australian bush they find the body of a dead Aboriginal girl in the river. Unwilling to abandon the trip they tie the body to a snag and continue to fish, only reporting the death days later. The secret to this film is the reactions to their experience from the diverse groups. It begins at the station when the policeman tells them 'we don't step over bodies for our recreational pursuits' and 'the whole town's ashamed of you'. When they are told to 'piss-off' from the station the press are waiting for them and Billy makes a comment that is "misinterpreted". Their shared experience changes them all and puts pressure on the various relationships and amongst themselves.

Poetry

At the Lunch Counter by Alden Nowlan

In this poem a fifteen year old girl taunts a blind boy at the lunch counter. She does this to impress other customers, especially the boys, who are watching and listening. In the end she wants them all to go away as she feels badly about her actions and wants to show her true kindness. Here we are privy to an experience from several perspectives and it casts much light on how people behave and their reactions to specific experiences. She lies to him about her appearance and also makes faces at the blind boy, Nathan. She immediately regrets her experience and to her credit learns from it and the poem concludes,

> 'Then,
> she stiffens and frowns
> wanting us to go away
> so she can be kind.'

Is this the human experience we see every day? Is this part of our human nature? The poet raises questions about the nature and response to human experiences.

Meditation on the A30 by John Betjemen

A middle aged man is driving along thinking about the angry quarrel he's had with his wife and his anger turns the car into a missile. It ends badly, 'And the corner's accepting its kill'. He is reflecting on a negative experience he has had earlier in the day and this experience has altered the way he sees his wife (She's losing her looks) and his response to all this negativity is to take it out on the other drivers and the manner of their driving. He searches his mind for something more than a wife who wants him dead (a nice blonde) but he cannot shake the anger from the experience and we know how it ends. Betjemen looks at modern living, the anger of experiences, and how these compound. Here the effect is completely negative, and this is the idea he is conveying.

Television Series

Westworld by Jonathan Nolan and Lisa Joy (2016)

Westworld is a highly acclaimed series based on the novel by Michael Creighton. *Westworld* isn't a typical amusement park and has been designed so that extremely wealthy vacationers can live out their fantasies. What makes this possible are the robotic 'hosts' that are programmed to provide the guests with anything they want including complete mayhem, murder and sex. Guests cannot be harmed, but as the show progresses we see these 'hosts' begin to evolve memory retention and a consciousness similar to the humans which control them. No plot spoilers here for this series, but what is of interest to us is that the experiences here where people can indulge all desires can lead down a dark path. Obviously there are consequences to this kind of behaviour and the all controlling Ford who runs the park is an ominously looming figure as he reconfigures the narratives. The series asks what it means to be human and how experiences shape and form lives – directly relevant to our study.

Louis Theroux's Weird Weekends (1998–2001)

A documentary series of which you might only need to watch one episode. In these episodes notorious documentarian Louis Theroux investigates and discovers different aspects of societies or groups within society. It is an unbiased look into the world of a vast variety of people, places, cultures and sub-cultures. Theroux aims to let these usually misunderstood people share their lives and experiences, whilst both Theroux and the viewer discover parts of society that is so separated and different from our regular lives. Watching how people's experiences shape their lives and impact on the way they are seen in the world is fascinating. Theroux is an experienced filmmaker and he is able to immerse himself in these people's lives and gives us an experience into fringe worlds. Have a look at the list of episodes and choose one that is of specific interest to you. Titles include *Black Nationalism*, *Survivalism* and *Looking for Love*.

Songs

Memories written by Brendon Urie, Spencer Smith, and John Fieldmann and performed by Panic! at the Disco (2011)

A song about nostalgia for the past, and the difficulties faced by young couples 'trying to make it on their own'. The song explores the experiences people have in relationships after the initial period of infatuation fades. The infatuation experience is common in teen romances and then reality and the pressures of the world invade the seemingly idyllic relationship. The singer holds a tone of regret throughout the song, as he recalls how hopeful the young couple were when their love began and how the difficulties of life and the resultant experiences can come between people. He sings 'You can't predict the end' after the initial 'inspired' decision that they could 'make it on their own'. Experience allows the relationship to 'fade away' despite them not wanting it to.

Roll Away Your Stone written and performed by Mumford and Sons (2009)

This song discusses the 'darkness' found within, and asks you to 'roll away your stone' and shed light onto the darkness. The singer begins by discussing the effects the darkness has on his life and on his relationships. The song ends, however on a positive note with the singer reclaiming his soul from the darkness, taking control of the direction of his life. We can only imagine the kind of experiences that lead to this kind of song and the despair that can sometimes enter the human experience. The singer acknowledges his loneliness in the modern world and how he is afraid 'of what he will discover inside'. The song is about acceptance and the damage of being judged without the full range of experiences being known.

Castle on the Hill written by Ed Sheeran (2017)

A song that recollects that the childhood friends you have and the shared experiences are the things that can shape your life. These shared experiences bind you with these people, and no matter what occurs in the next phase of your life these people are still relevant and loved. Despite what's happened in his life he 'can't wait to go home', and he states he misses the 'way you make me feel'. The songwriter notes the way he and his friends have changed but it makes no difference as he longs to see the 'castle on the hill' with his friends again. The song shows the importance of shared experiences and groups, especially in the formative years.

THE END

I hope this book has given you a good basis to unpack some of the key concepts in the Texts and Human Experiences module.

Good luck with your studies and the HSC.